Reflections on
STARTING
STRONG

A New
Teacher's
Journal

Skyhorse Publishing

Whatever you can do,
or believe you can,
begin it.
Boldness has genius,
power and magic in it.
—JOHANN WOLFGANG VON GOETHE

If your plan is for one year, plant rice;
If your plan is for ten years, plant trees;
If your plan is for a hundred years,
Educate children.

—CONFUCIUS

Nothing great was ever achieved without enthusiasm.

—RALPH WALDO EMERSON

Better than a thousand
days of diligent study
is one day with a
great teacher.

—JAPANESE PROVERB

The whole art of teaching is
only the art of awakening the
natural curiosity of young
minds for the purpose of
satisfying it afterwards.

—ANATOLE FRANCE

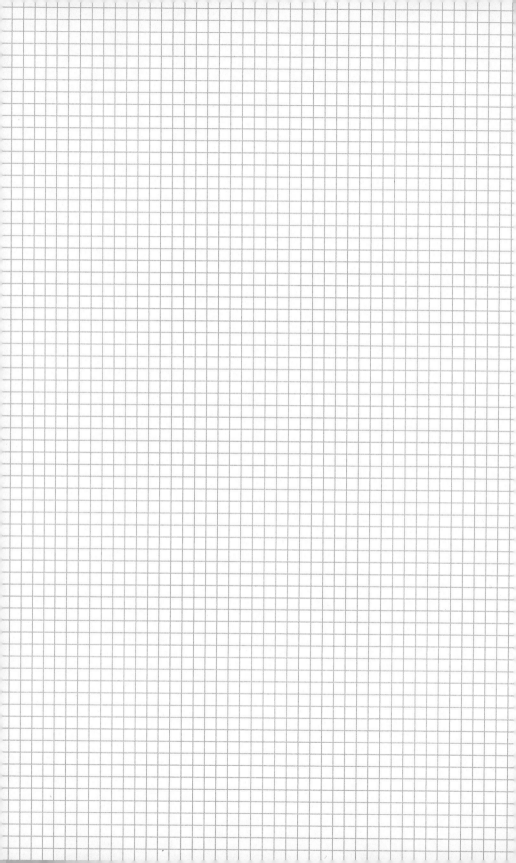

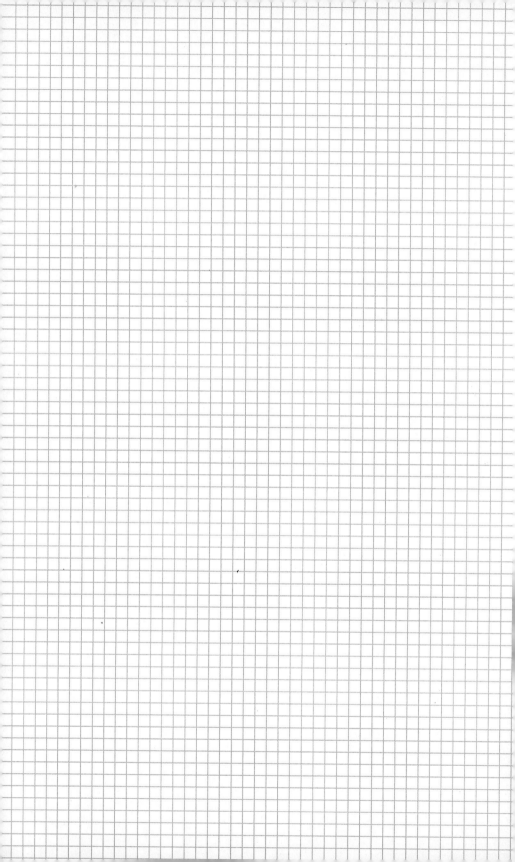

It is today that we create
the world of the future.
—ELEANOR ROOSEVELT

Education is not preparation for
life; education is life itself.

—JOHN DEWEY

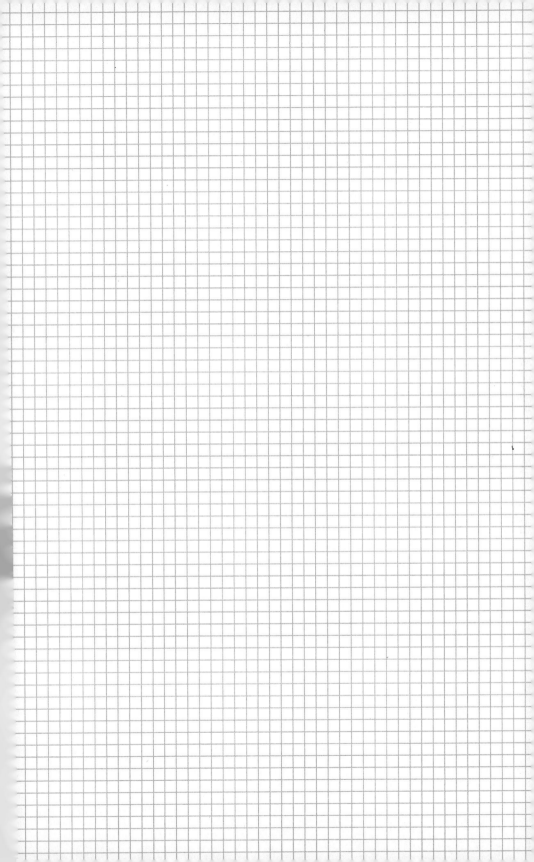

Education is not the filling of a
pail, but the lighting of a fire.

—W. B. YEATS

It is the supreme art of the teacher to awaken joy in creative expression and knowledge.

—ALBERT EINSTEIN

Instruction begins
when you, the
teacher, learn
from the learner;
put yourself in
his place so that
you may under-
stand . . . what
he learns and
the way he
understands it.

—SOREN KIERKEGAARD

A vision without a task is a dream.
A task without a vision is drudgery.
But a task with vision can change the world.

—BLACK ELK

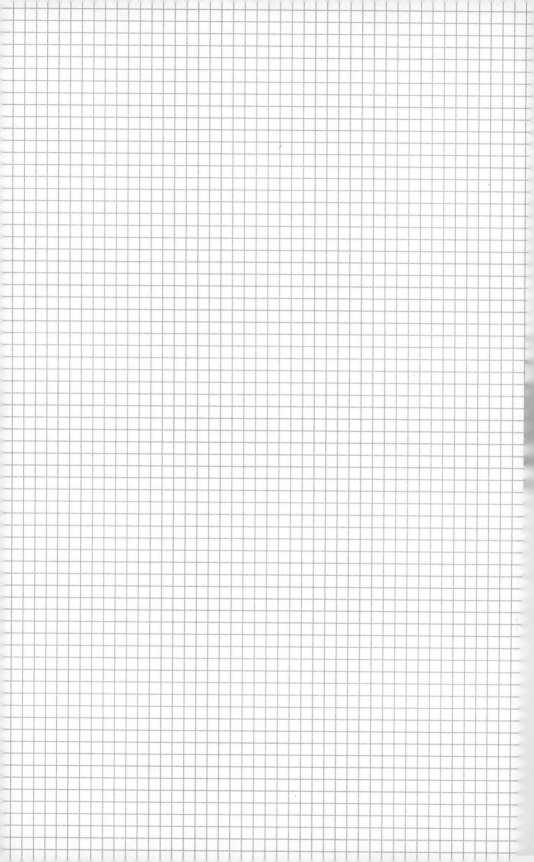

A teacher affects
eternity; he can
never tell where
his influence
stops.

—HENRY B. ADAMS

The teacher is one who made two ideas grow
where only one grew before.
—ELBERT HUBBARD

To raise new
questions, new
problems, to
regard old prob-
lems from a new
angle requires
creative imagi-
nation and
makes real
advances.

—ALBERT EINSTEIN

**Education is the key to unlock
the golden door of freedom.**
—GEORGE WASHINGTON CARVER

The secret of education lies in respecting the pupil.
—RALPH WALDO EMERSON

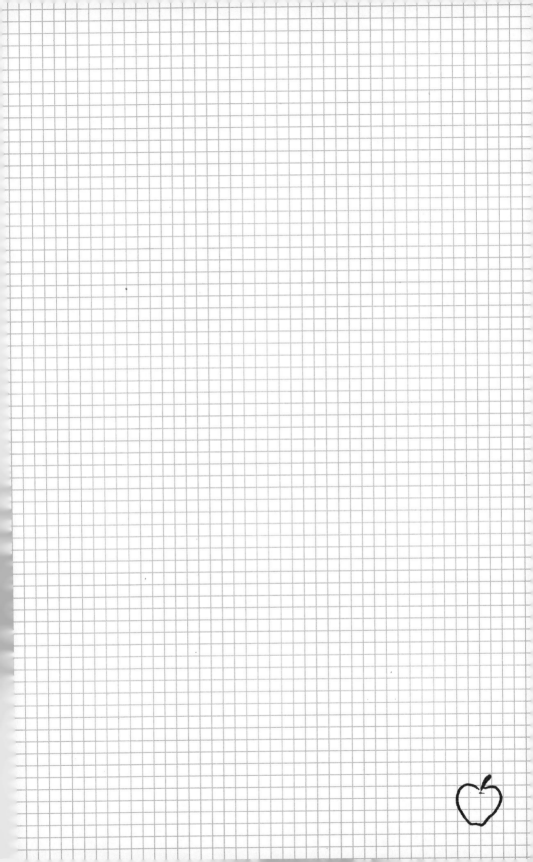

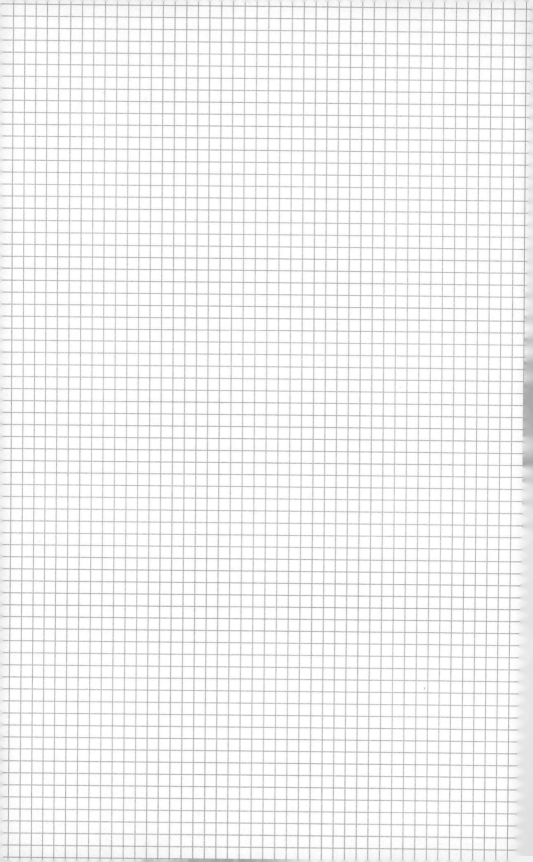

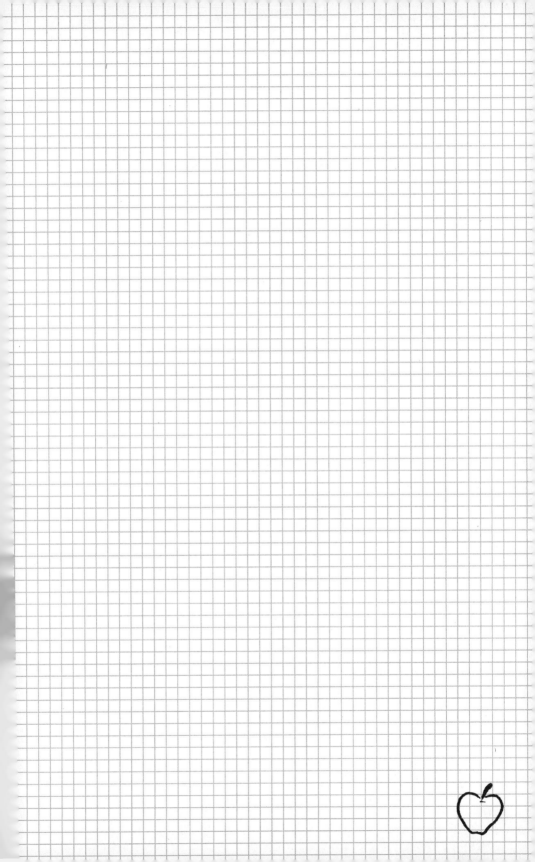

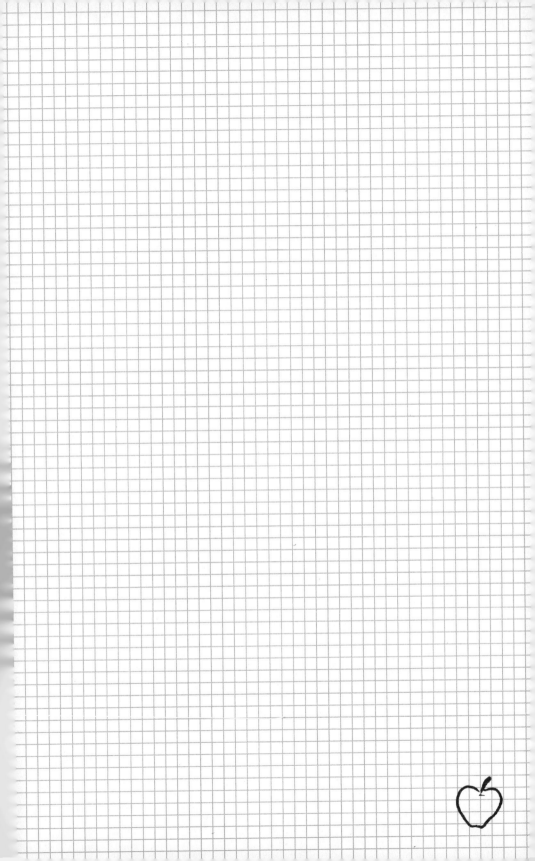

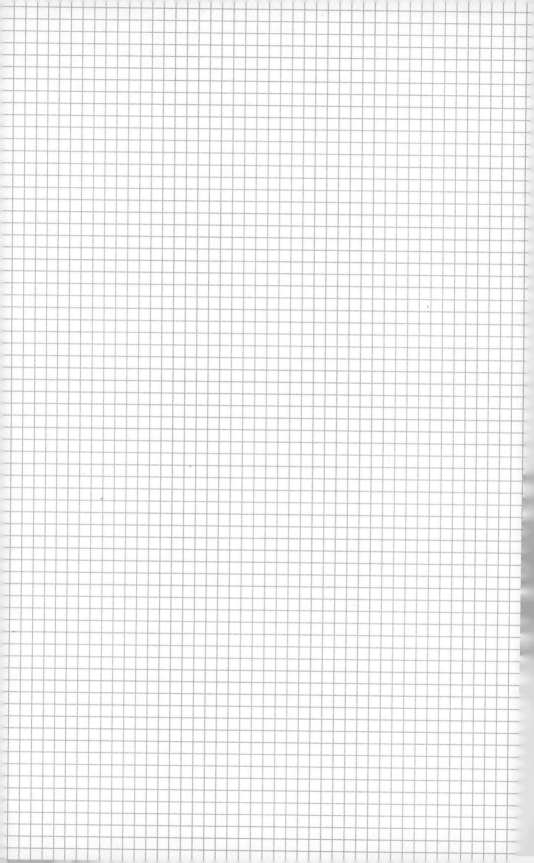

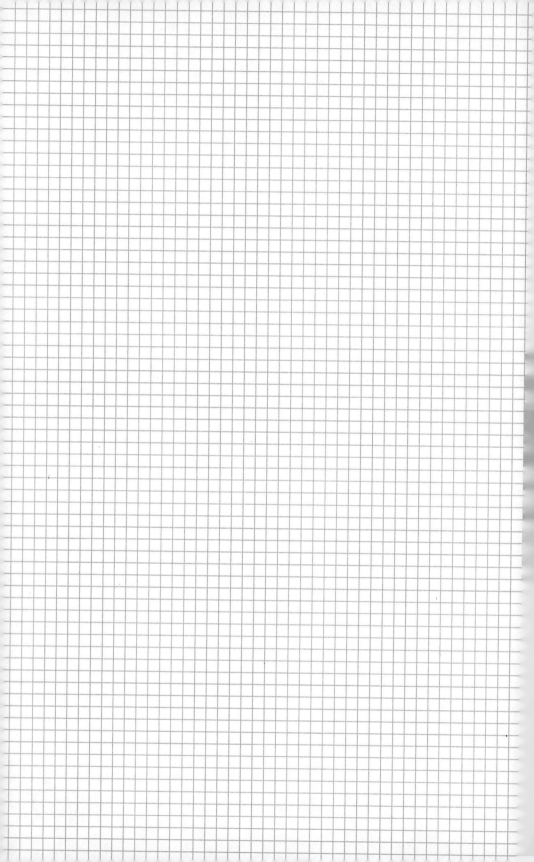

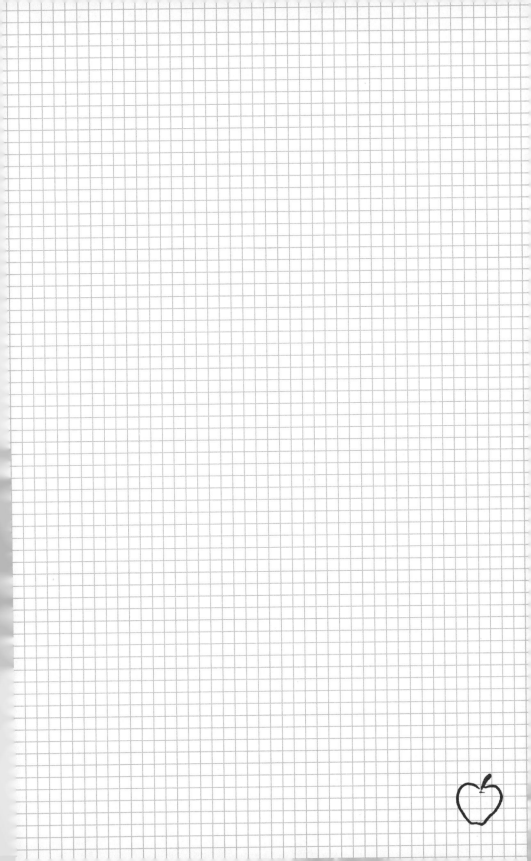

Every job is a self-portrait of the person who did it.
Autograph your work with excellence.

—UNKNOWN